Table of Contents

5 Bohemian Sunrise Table Runner

10 Coral Dreams Table Runner

14 Baby Ribbons Baby Blanket

19 Golden Pathways Throw

24 Welcome Home Baby Blanket

30 Annie's Throw

35 Aruba Sea Medallions

38 Pumpkin Spice Throw

42 Argyle Diamonds Throw

General Instructions, ***page 2***
Photo Index, ***page 48***

Baby Ribbons Baby Blanket, ***page 14***

Pumpkin Spice Throw, ***page 38***

Bohemian Sunrise Table Runner, ***page 5***

Meet the Designer

Trice Boerens has worked for many years in the quilting, needlework and paper industries. Along with designing projects for best-selling books and kits, she has also worked as a photo stylist, an art director and a creative editor.

The designs for this book were inspired by treasures that she uncovered in antique stores, flea markets and attics.

General Instructions

Monk's cloth weaving is a large-scale form of embroidery done on monk's cloth. A loosely woven even-weave, this fabric is 100 percent cotton and available in a variety of colors. Although the threads are represented by only two threads on the pattern graphs, the surface texture is made of four horizontal and four vertical threads. The four vertical threads are referred to as a "float." The needle is inserted under the floats only, and as a result the thread does not appear on the back of the fabric. One project, however, the Welcome Home Baby Blanket on page 24, features a running stitch. This requires the needle to be inserted through a hole at the float intersections and drawn to the back of the fabric. Then it is inserted again and drawn to the front. In this particular case the yarn will appear on the back of the fabric.

Starting at the center of the fabric, each length of yarn is worked from edge to edge with no breaks. For right-handed weavers, the rows are worked from right to left. For left-handed weavers it is the opposite.

Materials

Monk's cloth: 2½ yds for throws, 1⅔ yds for baby blankets, 30 inches x 72 inches for table runners

Needle: #13 yarn needle

Yarn: 4-ply medium (worsted) weight

Safety pins: Use pins to mark the center point and design starting points.

Preparing the Fabric

The fabric will quickly unravel if the cut edges are not secured. For throws and baby blankets, machine zigzag-stitch along cut edges (top and bottom). For table runners, machine zigzag-stitch around all edges.

It is necessary to preshrink the fabric so it will hold the yarn in place. Machine wash with detergent in warm to hot water and dry completely. Since it is 100 percent cotton, there will be a considerable amount of shrinkage. The natural version will shrink more than the white or the colored fabrics.

Cutting the Yarn

Yarn is measured according to the width of the fabric. For example, two widths is one strand that is twice as long as the fabric is wide.

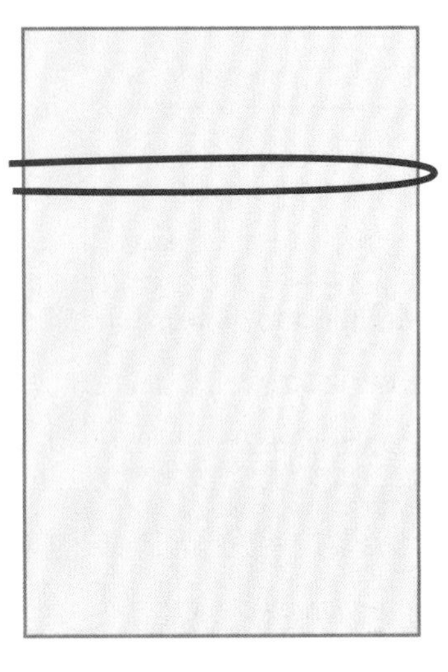

Cutting Yarn

Weaving

1. To find the center of the fabric, fold the cloth in half vertically and then in half horizontally. Place a safety pin in the center float to mark the center of fabric.

2. Cut yarn to the length specified in the pattern and thread the needle. Slide the needle under the marked float and draw up the yarn until the float is at the center of the length.

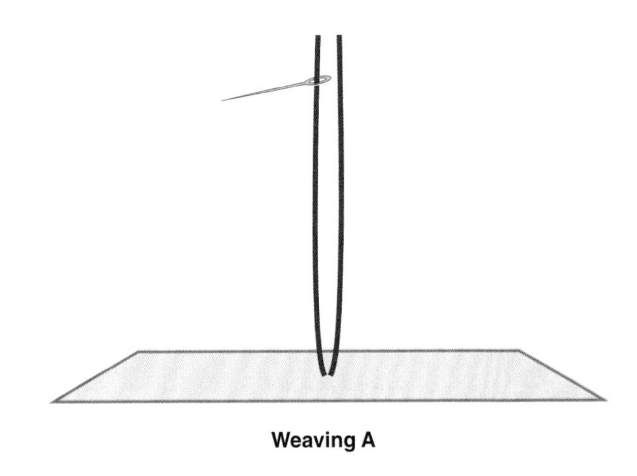

Weaving A

3. Find the center of the design on the chart and weave from the center of the fabric to the left edge. Maintain an even tension while weaving. Make one small stitch in the selvage edge to secure the yarn. If there is no selvage edge, loop the yarn through the last float twice to secure the yarn.

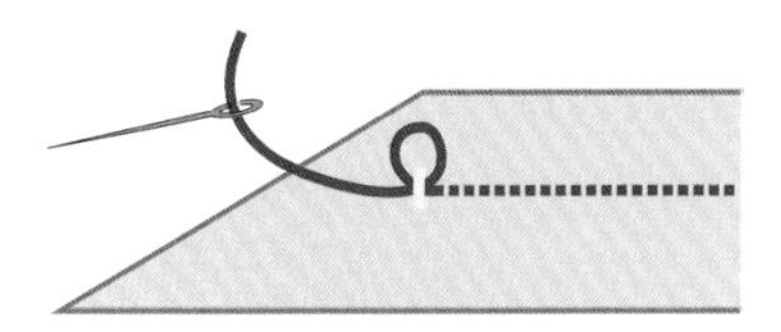

Weaving B

4. Trim the yarn end. Turn the fabric and the pattern upside down, and weave to the opposite edge. Secure the yarn and trim the end.

5. Repeat with the remaining yarn lengths.

Note: *A float with an asterisk accommodates two strands of yarn.*

Stitch Diagrams

Note: *Not all stitches are represented here. Carefully follow each individual pattern chart and count horizontal and vertical rows before inserting the needle.*

Running Stitch

Diagonal Running Stitch

Step-Up One

Step-Up One and a Half
One vertical thread to the left.

Step-Up One and a Half
One vertical thread to the right.

Step-Up Two

Figure Eight Up One
Outlined thread sits on top.

Figure Eight Up Two
Outlined thread sits on top.

Finishing

Fringe edges for throws

1. Machine zigzag-stitch along the selvage edges. Use a stitch that is small enough to catch the yarn in the stitching, then trim the yarn ends.

2. On the top and bottom of the throw, zigzag-stitch along the desired rows.

3. Trim the edge a few rows from the stitching line and pull the horizontal threads to create fringe.

Fringe edges for table runners

1. Machine zigzag-stitch several rows in from the edges. Trim the yarn ends.

2. Trim the edges a few rows from the stitching line and pull the threads to create fringe.

Bias binding for baby blankets

1. Machine zigzag-stitch around the outside edges. Trim the yarn ends.

2. Sew premade bias binding around the outside edges of the afghan, covering the zigzag stitching. Fold the binding at each corner to create a mitered "joint."

3. Overlap bias ends.

4. Fold the binding to the back and hand-slip stitch the folded edge to secure. ❖

Binding A

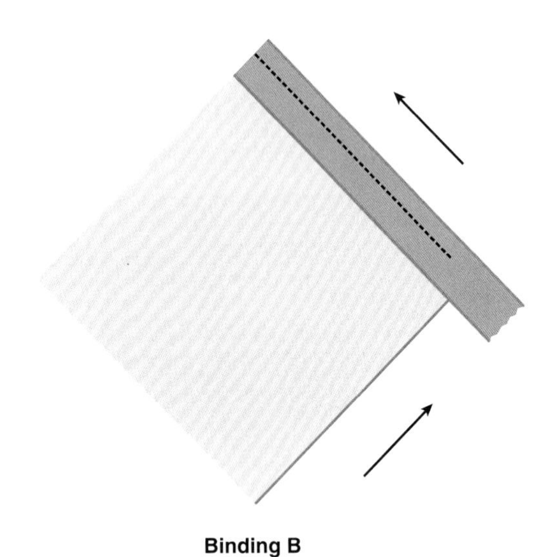

Binding B

Binding C

Binding D

Bohemian Sunrise Table Runner

Add a dramatic flair to your table setting with the bright and bold colors of the Bohemian Sunrise Table Runner.

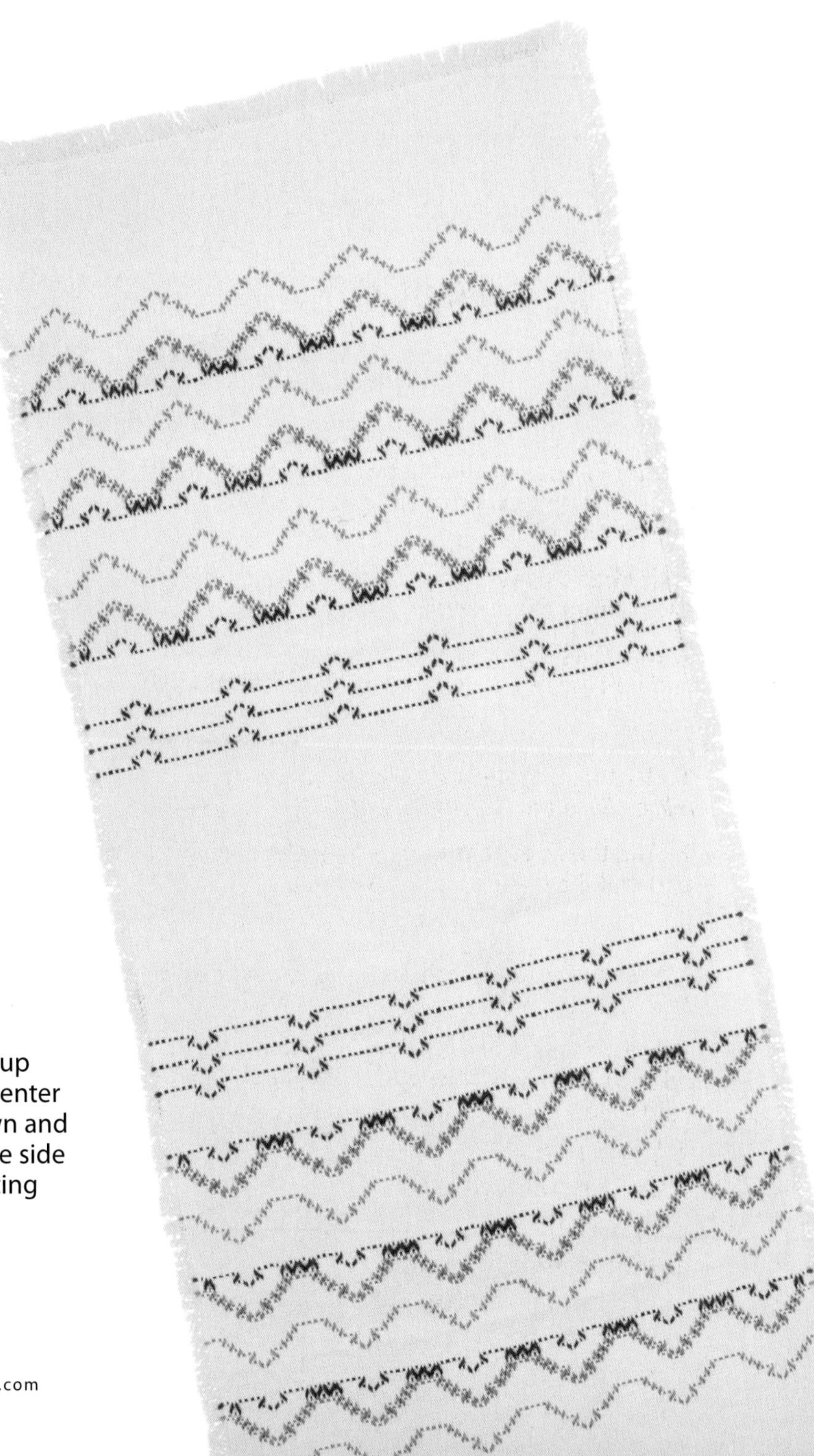

Skill Level
Easy

Finished Size
22 inches x 53 inches

Materials
- Monk's cloth:
  30 inches x 72 inches white
- Red Heart Super Saver medium (worsted) weight yarn (7 oz/364 yds/ 198g per skein):
  1 skein each #390 hot red, #528 medium purple and #254 pumpkin
- #13 yarn needle

Pattern Notes
Refer to General Instructions for preparing monk's cloth and for stitching information.

Instructions
1. For each center accent band you will need the following yarn lengths:
3 hot red—2 fabric widths

For each design band you will need the following yarn lengths:
1 hot red—2 fabric widths
2 medium purple—2 fabric widths
1 pumpkin—2 fabric widths

2. Mark fabric center. Referring to Chart A on page 8 and counting 20 floats (40 rows total) up from center, weave 1 length of hot red from center of Row 1 to side edge. Turn fabric upside down and weave remaining yarn from center to opposite side edge. Repeat with remaining 2 rows, completing center accent band.

3. Allowing 4 rows of floats (8 rows total) between design bands and referring to Chart B on page 9, work 3 design bands on fabric below center accent band. Work bands on opposite half of fabric in same manner.

4. Refer to General Instructions for finishing techniques and finish as desired. ❖

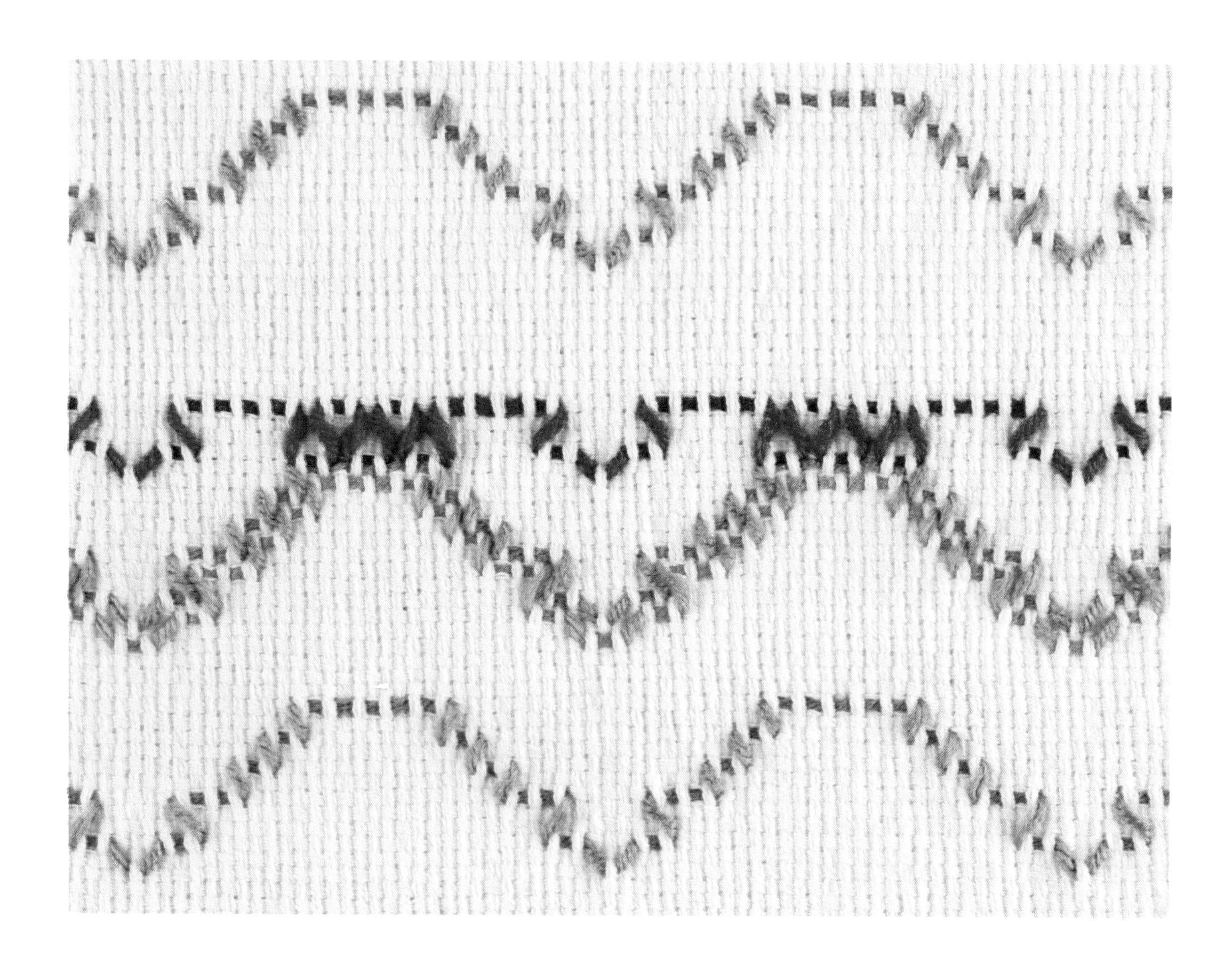

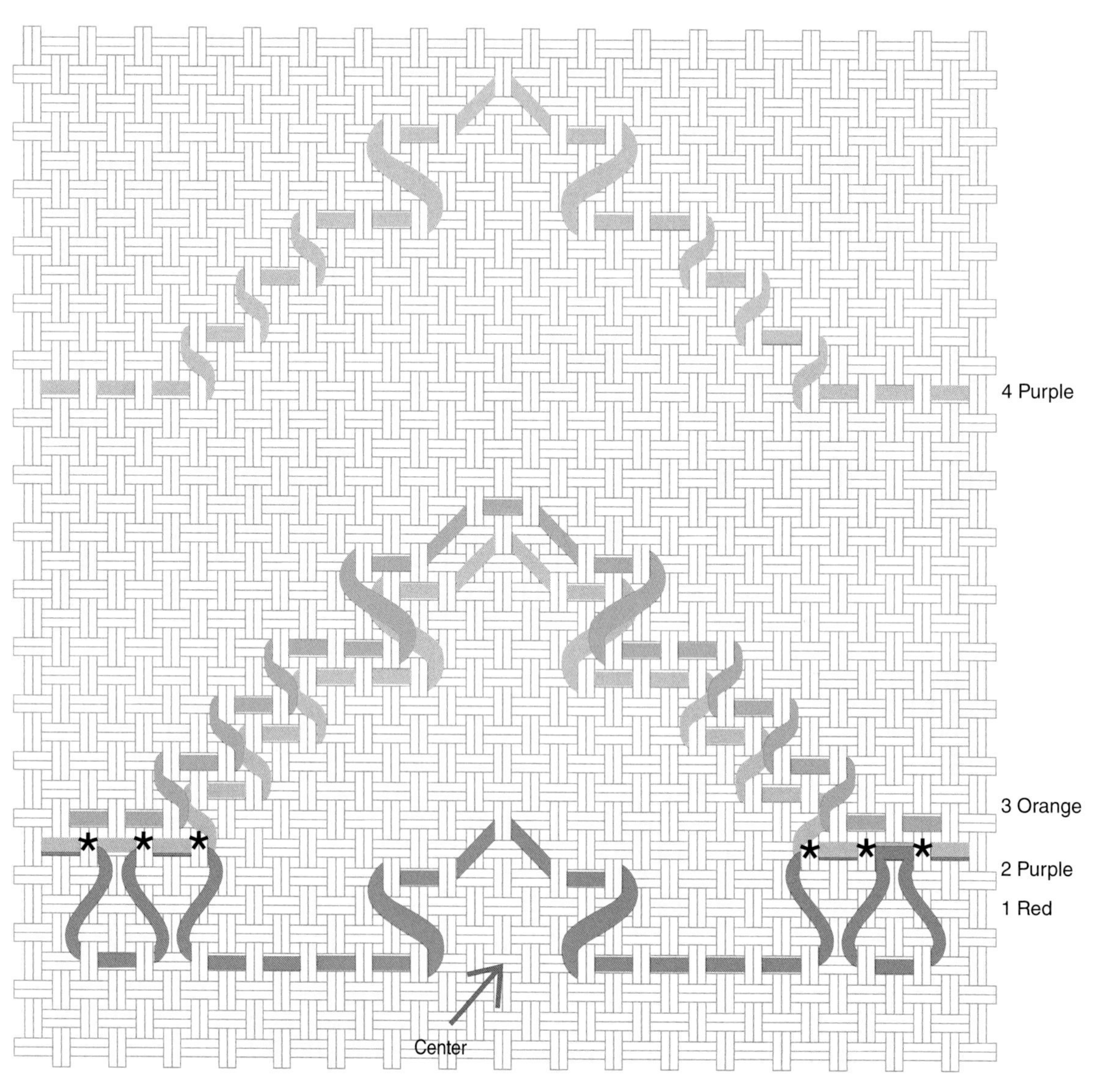

Chart A

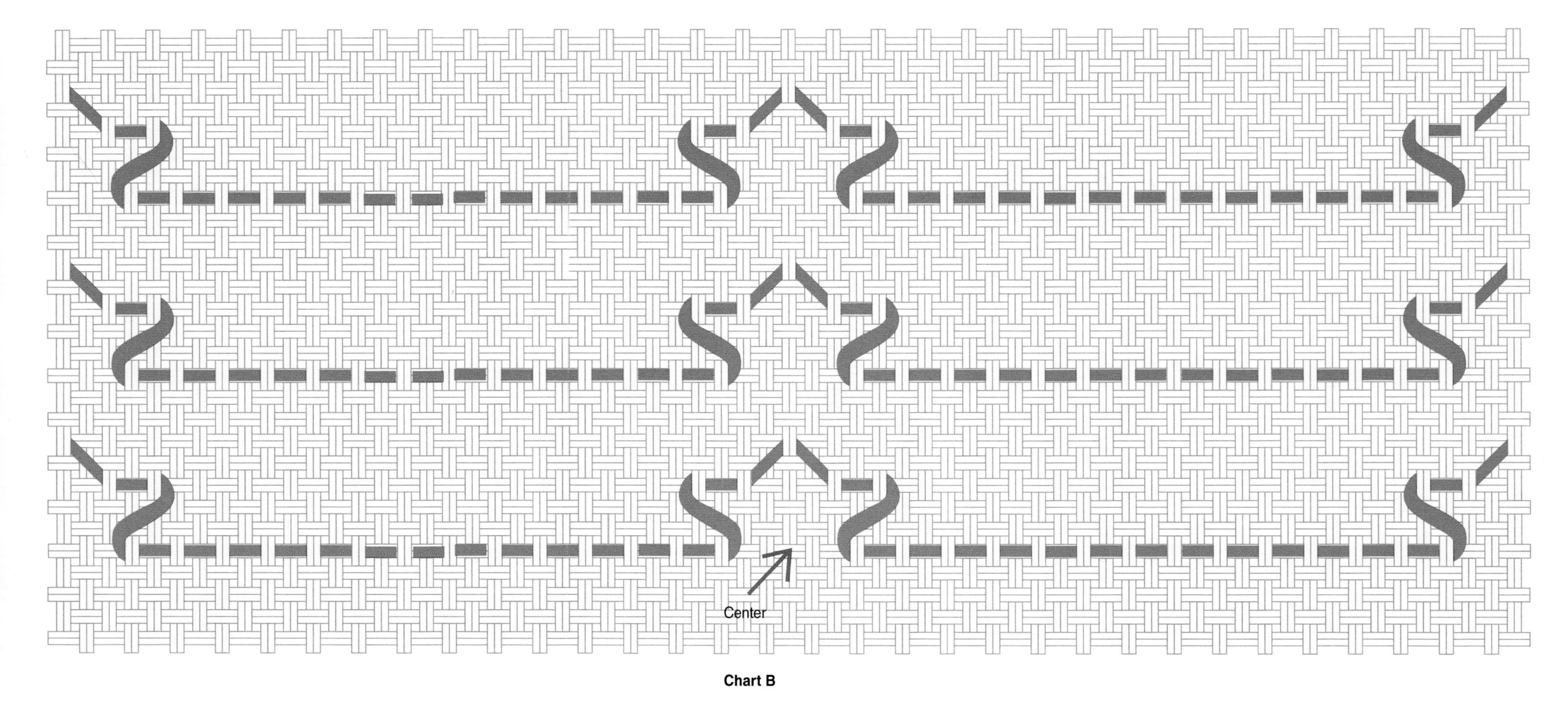

Chart B

Coral Dreams Table Runner

Dress up your table with the warm tones of this lovely table runner.

Skill Level
Easy

Finished Size
23 inches x 56 inches

Materials
- Monk's cloth:
  30 inches x 72 inches white
- Red Heart Super Saver medium (worsted) weight yarn (7 oz/364 yds/198g per skein):
  1 skein each #327 light coral and #330 linen
- #13 yarn needle

Pattern Notes
Refer to General Instructions for preparing monk's cloth and for stitching information.

Instructions
1. For each design band you will need the following yarn lengths:
6 light coral—2½ fabric widths (for Rows 1–3)
2 light coral—3½ fabric widths (for Row 4)
2 linen—2 fabric widths

2. Mark fabric center. Referring to chart on page 12, and beginning 32 floats down from center, weave 1 length of light coral from center of Row 1 to side edge. Turn fabric upside down and weave remaining yarn from center to opposite side edge.

3. Noting overlaps, repeat with remaining rows. Turn chart upside down and weave next 5 rows to complete design band.

4. Allowing 20 rows of floats (21 rows total) between design bands, work 2nd design band on fabric below first design band. Repeat design bands on opposite half of fabric.

5. Refer to General Instructions for finishing techniques and finish as desired. ❖

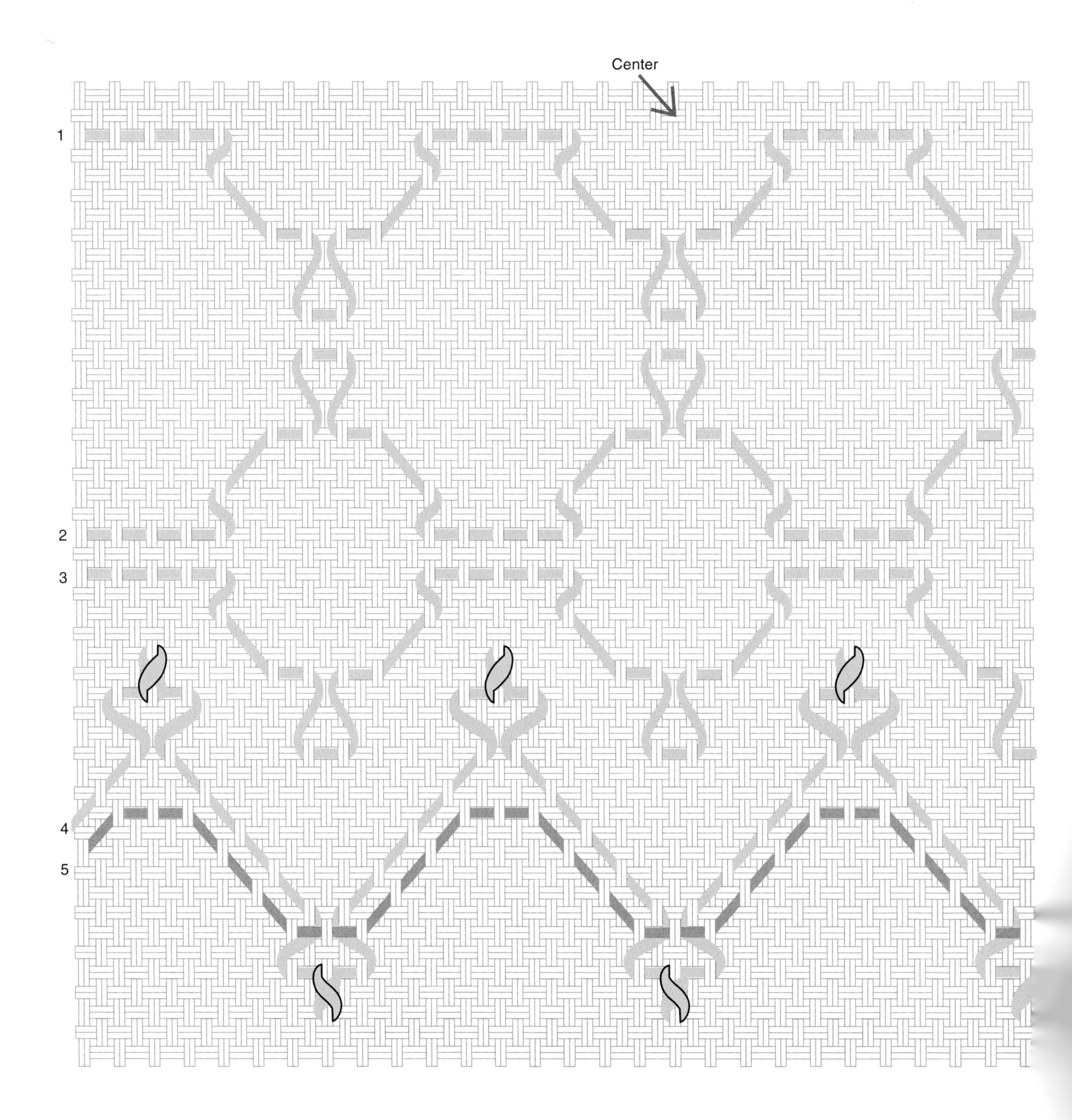
Center
1
2
3
4
5

Baby Ribbons Baby Blanket

Stitch this beautiful baby blanket and give as a gift to the new parents. It's a gift they will treasure for years to come.

Skill Level
Easy

Finished Size
23 inches x 56 inches

Materials
- Monk's cloth:
  1⅔ yds natural
- Red Heart Super Saver medium (worsted) weight yarn (7 oz/364 yds/198g per skein):
  1 skein each #347 light periwinkle, #672 spring green, #505 Aruba sea and #373 petal pink
- #13 yarn needle

Pattern Notes
Refer to General Instructions for preparing monk's cloth and for stitching information.

Instructions
1. For each design band A you will need the following yarn lengths:
4 light periwinkle—2½ fabric widths
1 spring green—3½ fabric widths

For each design band B you will need the following yarn lengths:
4 Aruba sea—2½ fabric widths
1 petal pink—3½ fabric widths

2. Mark fabric center. Referring to chart on page 16, weave 1 length of spring green from center of Row 1 to side edge. Turn fabric upside down and weave remaining yarn from center to opposite side edge. With light periwinkle, weave remaining 4 rows to complete design band A.

3. Allowing 8 rows of floats (17 rows total) between design bands, work band B and then design band A. Repeat design bands on opposite half of fabric.

4. Refer to General Instructions for finishing techniques and finish as desired. ❖

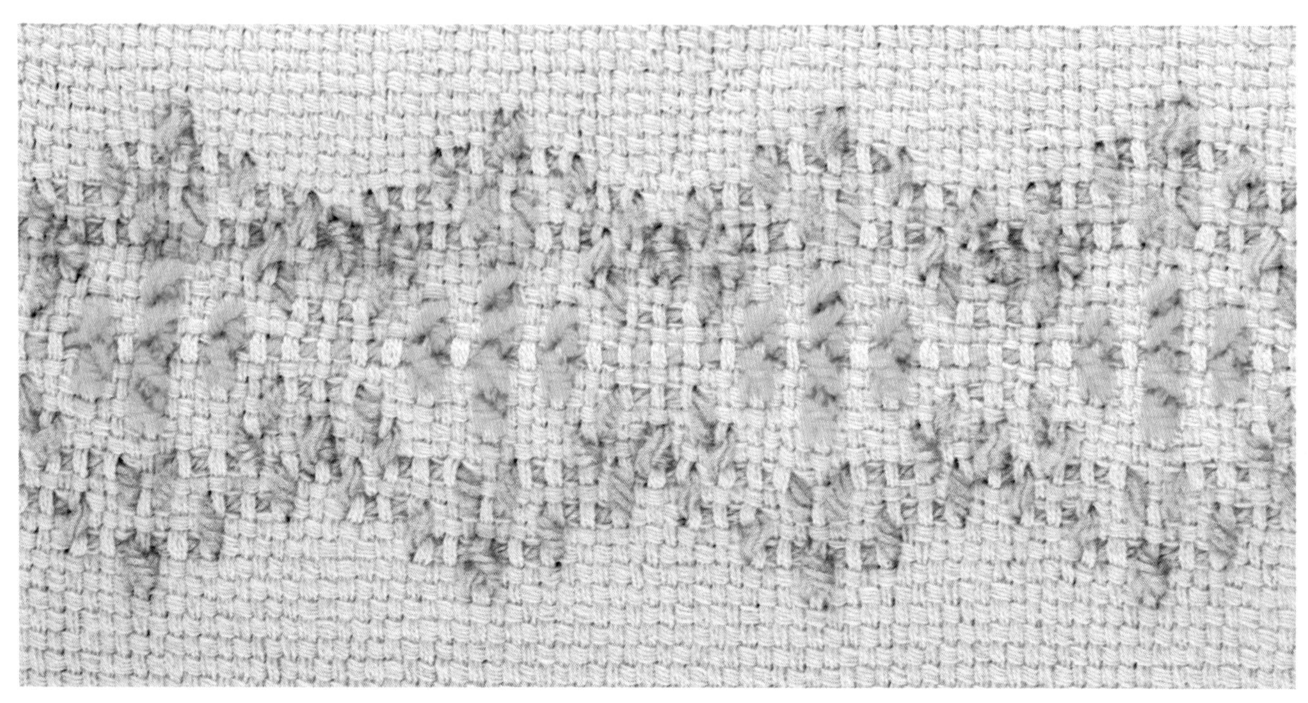

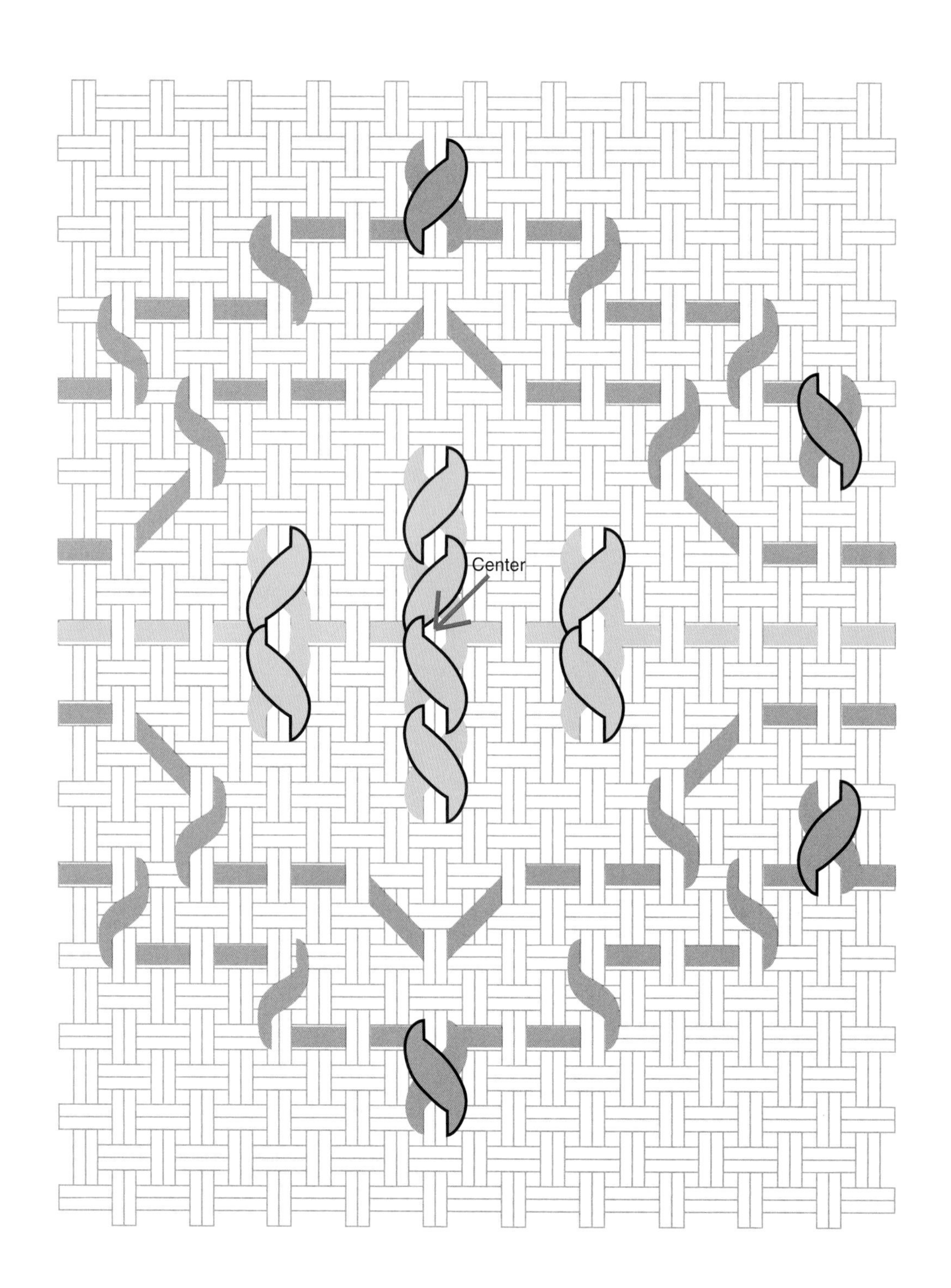
Center

Monk's Cloth for Toda

Golden Pathways Throw

Stitch this beautiful throw as a gift or donate it to your favorite fundraising charity.

Skill Level
Easy

Finished Size
48 inches x 68 inches

Materials
- Monk's cloth:
  2½ yds natural
- Red Heart Super Saver medium (worsted) weight yarn (7 oz/364 yds/198g per skein):
  1 skein each #321 gold and #505 Aruba sea
- #13 yarn needle

Pattern Notes
Refer to General Instructions for preparing monk's cloth and for stitching information.

Instructions
1. For each plain design band in the afghan center, you will need the following yarn lengths:
2 gold—3½ fabric widths
2 Aruba sea—2 fabric widths

For each filled design band on afghan ends, you will need:
2 gold—3½ fabric widths
4 Aruba sea—2 fabric widths

For the filler rows on afghan ends, you will need:
2 Aruba sea—2 fabric widths

2. Mark fabric center. Referring to chart on page 22, weave 1 length of gold from center of Row 1 to side edge. Turn fabric upside down and weave remaining yarn from center to opposite side edge. Following chart, weave 1 length of Aruba sea for Row 2. Do not work Row 3 at this time.

3. Turn chart upside down and weave next 2 rows to complete design band. Note that floats with asterisks accommodate 2 strands of yarn.

4. Allowing 0 rows of floats (1 row total) between design bands, weave adjoining rows to create a staggered pattern. To stagger pattern, shift it left or right to 1 half repeat, and align short ends of rectangles (see diagram 1). Note that after shifting pattern, weave only half of design band (1 gold and 1 Aruba sea). Repeat with remaining rows, having 2 plain design bands and 4 filled design bands on either side of center band.

5. Weave Aruba sea following Row 3 on chart for filler rows at end of throw as desired. Since yarn lengths are incorporated into throw ends only, the filler rows are represented as a darker value.

6. Refer to General Instructions for finishing techniques and finish as desired. ❖

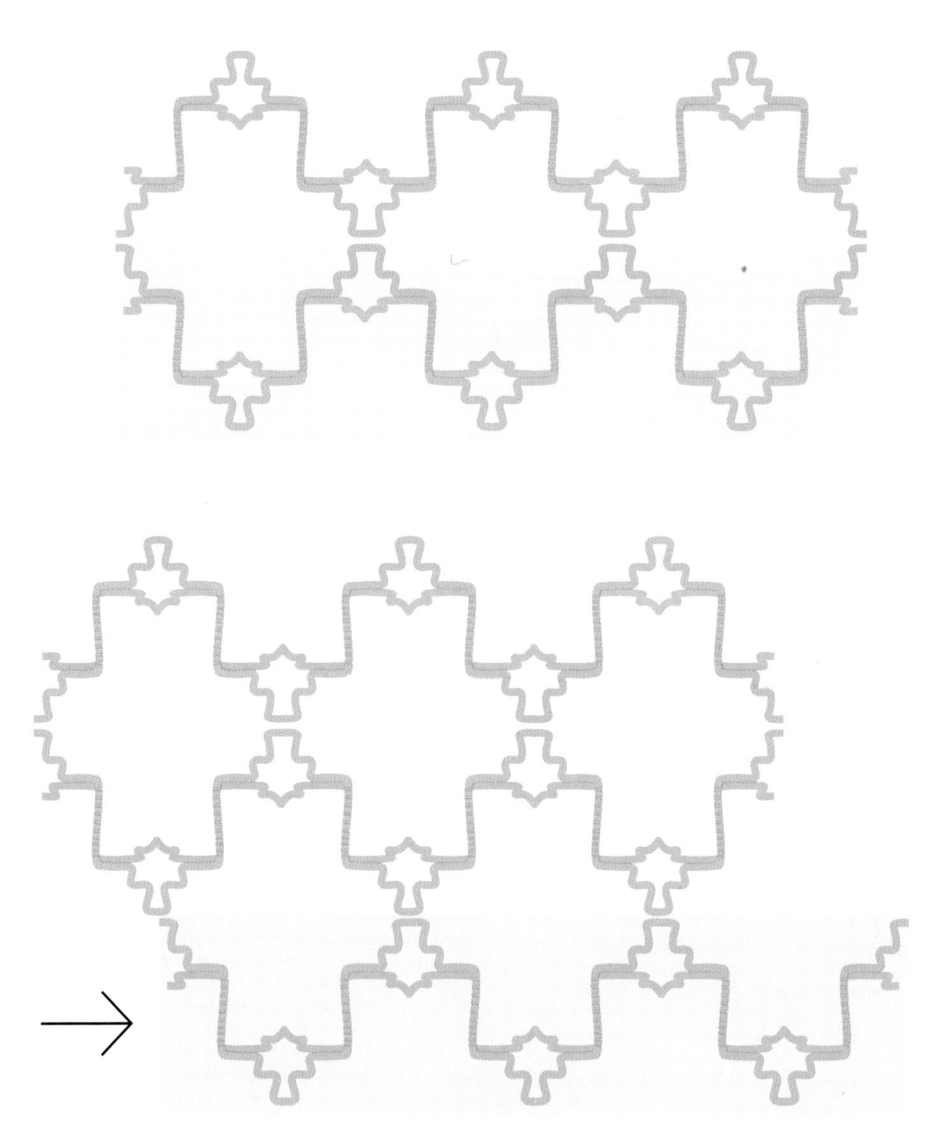

Diagram 1

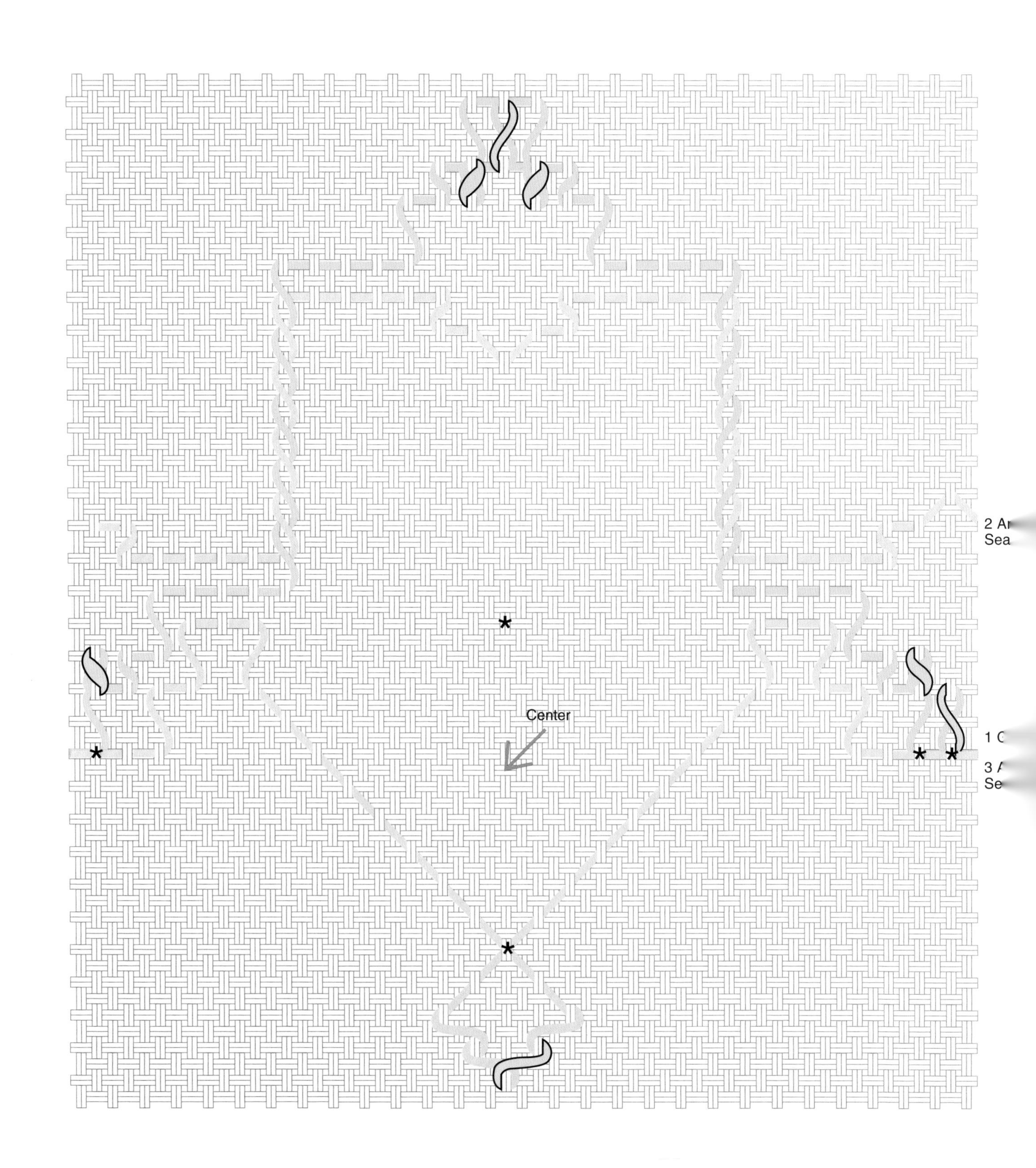
Center
2 A
Sea
1 C
3 A
Se

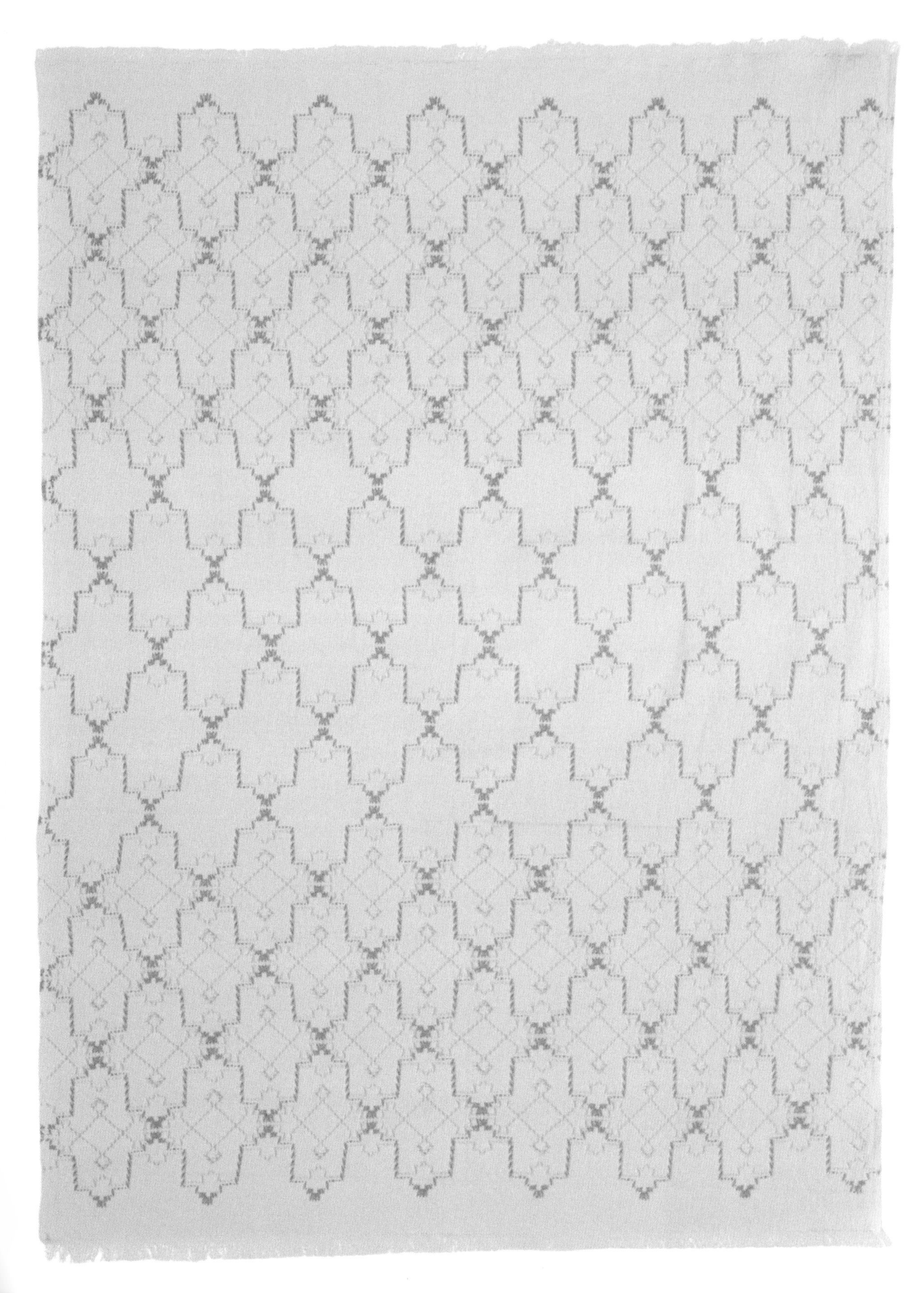

Welcome Home Baby Blanket

Welcome home the new baby with the soft colors and pretty design of this baby blanket.

Skill Level
Easy

Finished Size
47 inches x 47 inches

Materials
- Monk's cloth:
  1⅔ yds white
- Red Heart Super Saver medium (worsted) weight yarn (7 oz/364 yds/ 198g per skein):
  1 skein each #505 Aruba sea
  and #327 light coral
- #13 yarn needle

Pattern Notes
Refer to General Instructions for preparing monk's cloth and for stitching information.

1. For each design band you will need the following yarn lengths:
2 Aruba sea—2 fabric widths

For coral accents:
2 light coral—1½ fabric widths

2. Mark fabric center. Referring to Chart A on page 26, weave 1 length of Aruba sea from center to side edge. Turn fabric upside down and weave remaining yarn from center to opposite side edge. Referring to Chart B on page 27, weave 1 length of light coral for coral accent. Repeat for 2nd coral accent.

3. Following charts and alternating plain design bands with design bands with coral accents, work 9 design bands on either side of center design band.

4. Refer to General Instructions for finishing techniques and finish as desired. ❖

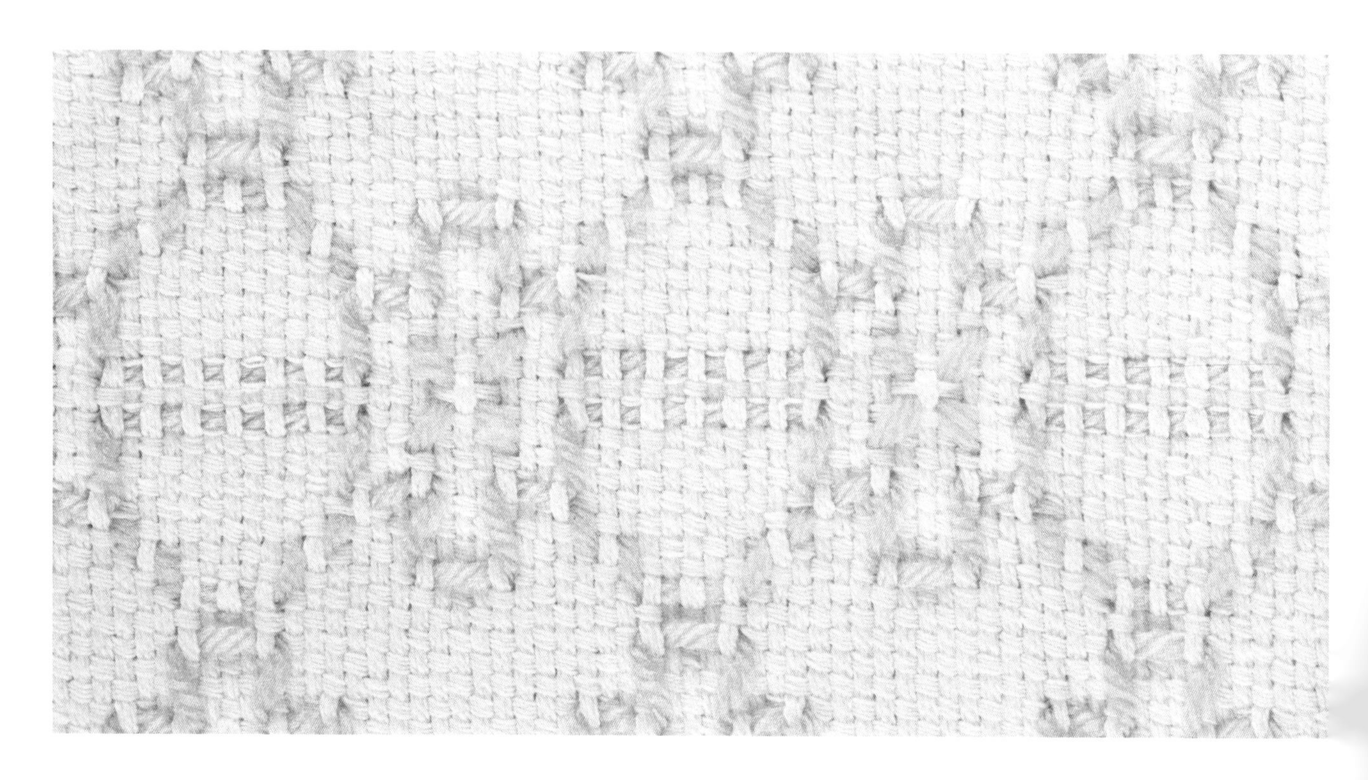

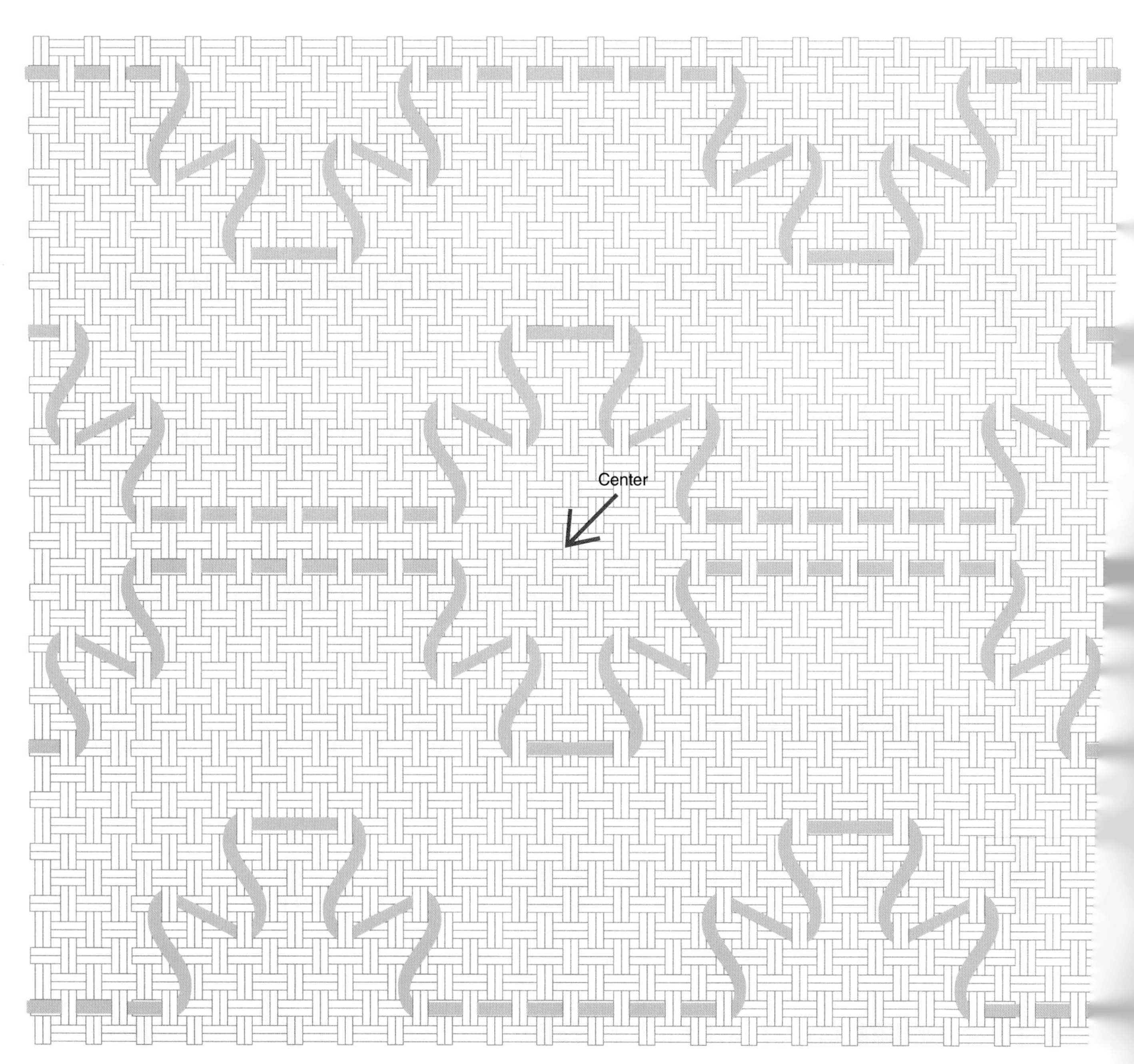

Chart A

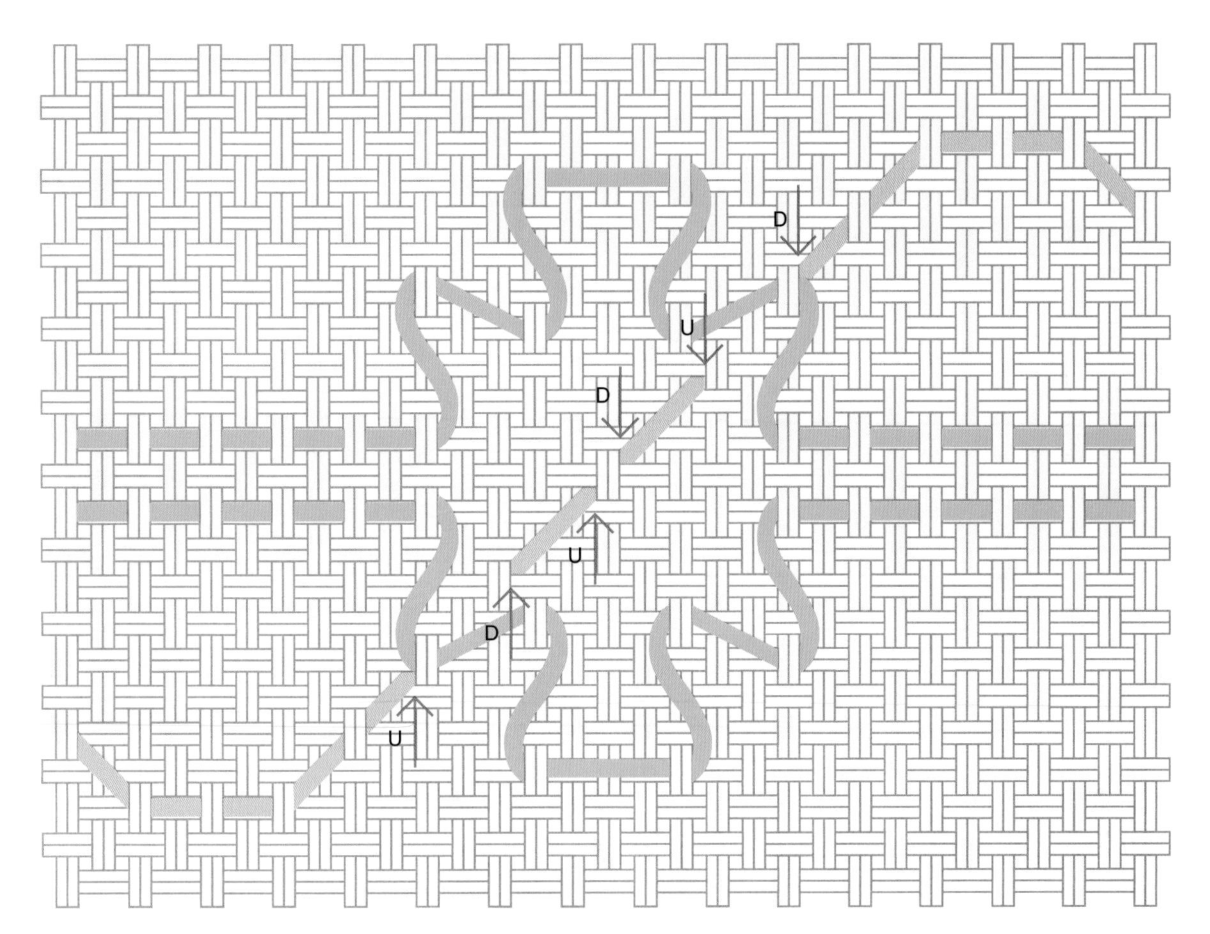

D - down to the back of the fabric
U - up to the front of the fabric

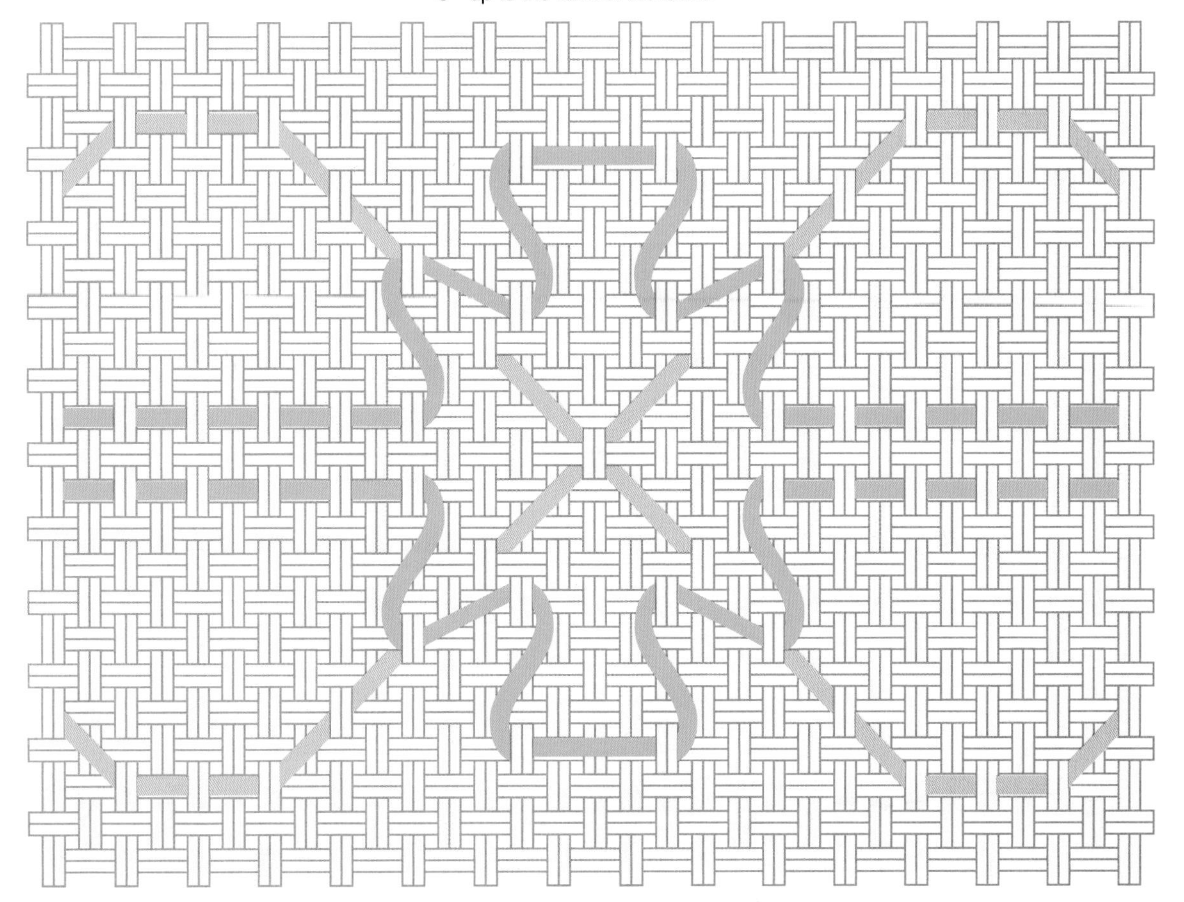

Chart B

Annie's Throw

Stitched with rose and gray, this throw is versatile for any room of the home. Change the yarn colors to match your special decor.

Skill Level
Easy

Finished Size
48 inches x 64 inches

Materials
- Monk's cloth:
  2½ yds natural
- Annie's Choice medium (worsted) weight yarn (7 oz/328 yds/198g per skein):
  1 skein each #AC1001 teaberry rose and #AC1015 stormy
- #13 yarn needle

Pattern Notes
Refer to General Instructions for preparing monk's cloth and for stitching information.

Instructions
1. For each design band you will need the following yarn lengths:
6 teaberry rose—3½ fabric widths
2 stormy—2 fabric widths

2. Mark fabric center. Referring to Chart A on page 32, weave 1 length of teaberry rose from center of Row 1 to side edge. Turn fabric upside down and weave remaining yarn from center to opposite side edge. Since the lengths overlap, the first row is represented as a lighter value.

3. Noting overlaps, follow sequence indicated on charts and repeat with remaining rows. Turn charts upside down and weave next 4 rows to complete design band. The floats with asterisks accommodate 2 strands of yarn.

4. Allowing 5 rows of floats (11 rows total) between design bands, work 4 additional design bands, 2 on each side of first design band.

5. Refer to General Instructions for finishing techniques and finish as desired. ❖

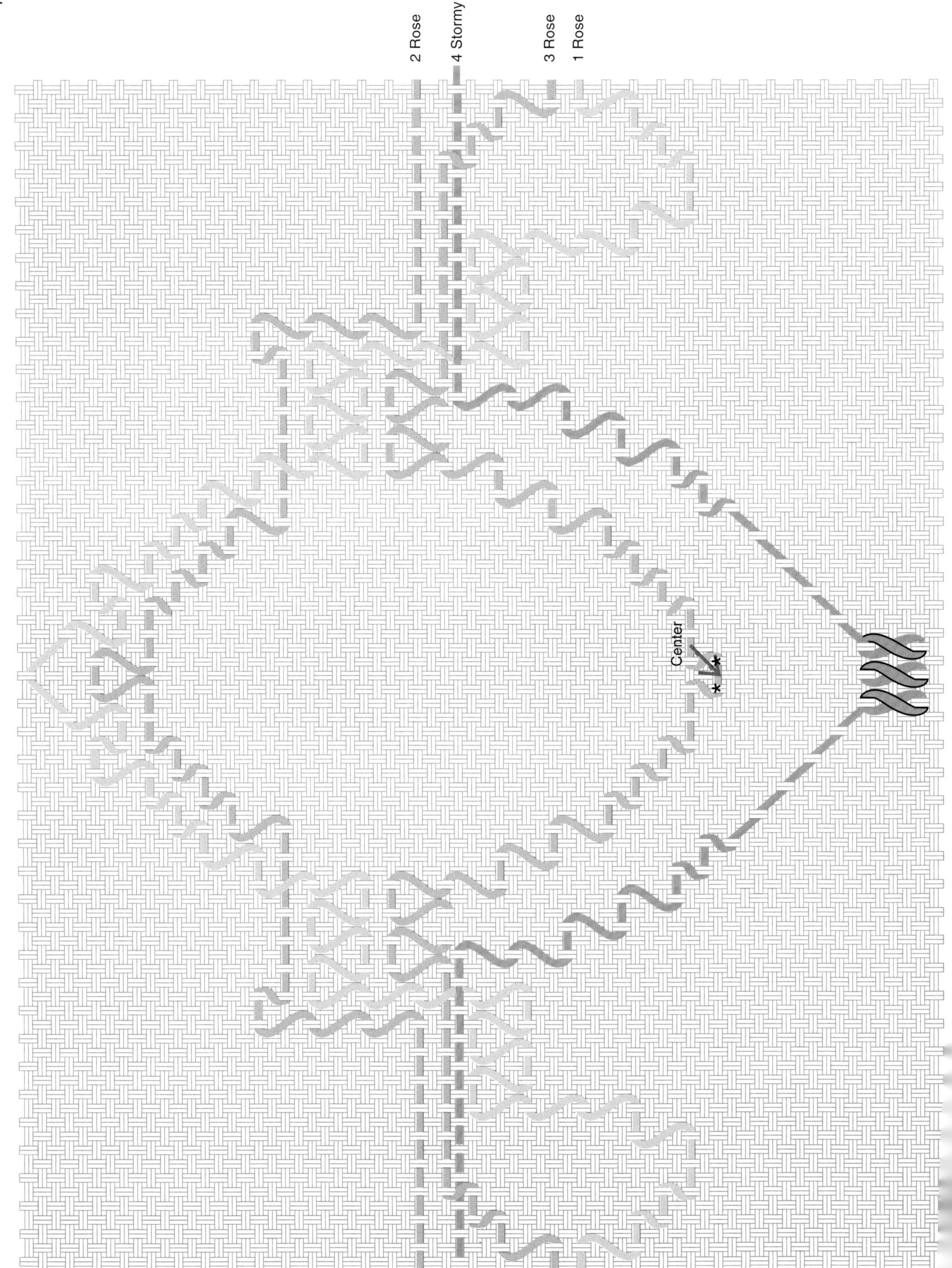
2 Rose
4 Stormy
3 Rose
1 Rose
Center

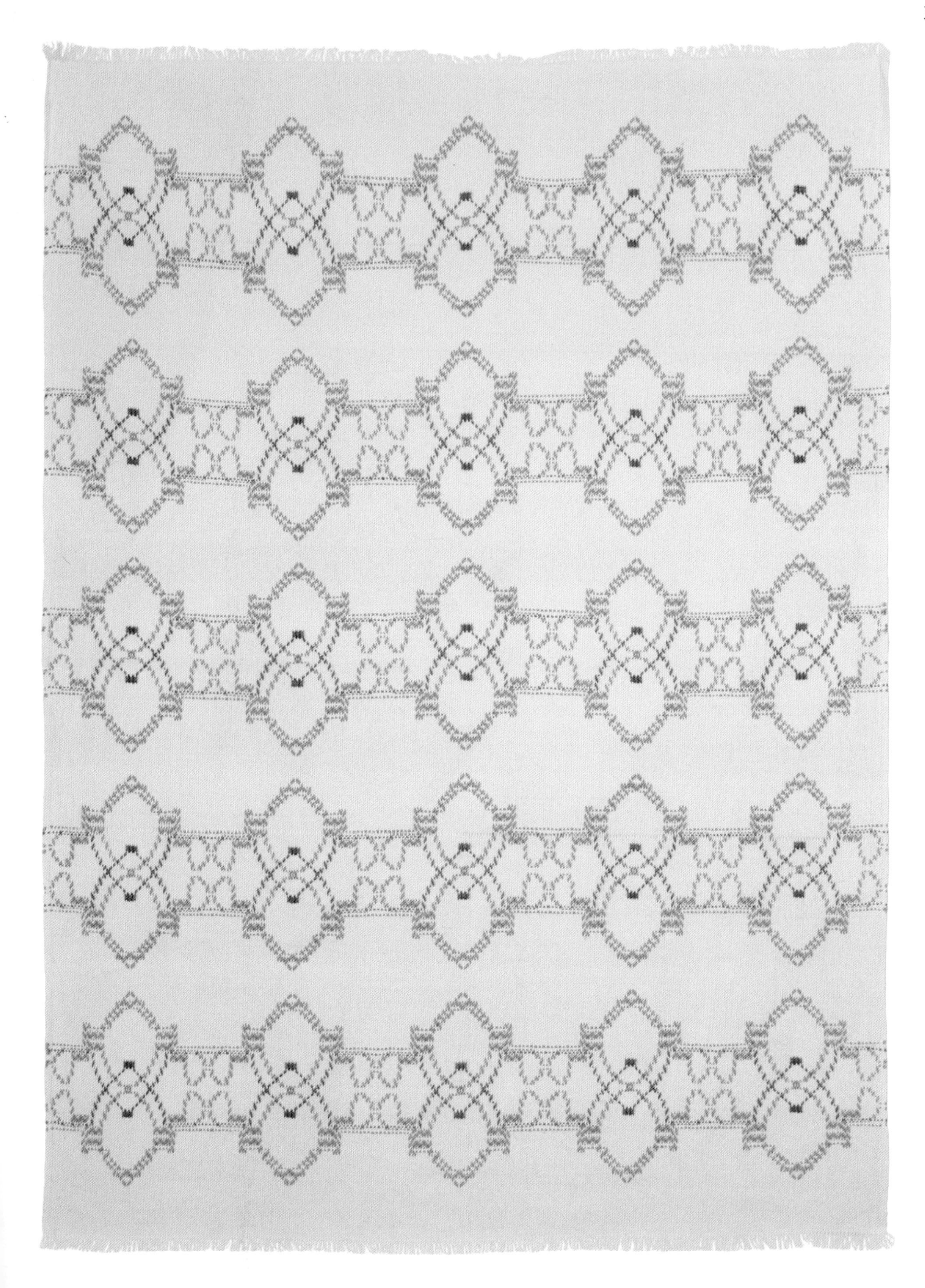

Aruba Sea Medallions

Wrap yourself up in this beautiful sea of tranquility.
If you listen closely, you may be able to hear the ocean.

Skill Level
Easy

Finished Size
48 inches x 68 inches

Materials
- Monk's cloth:
  2½ yds natural
- Red Heart Super Saver medium (worsted) weight yarn (7 oz/364 yds/198g per skein):
  1 skein each #505 Aruba sea, #656 real teal, #381 light blue and #320 cornmeal
- #13 yarn needle

Pattern Notes
Refer to General Instructions for preparing monk's cloth and for stitching information.

Instructions
1. For each design band you will need the following yarn lengths:
6 Aruba sea—3 fabric widths
2 real teal—3 fabric widths
2 light blue—3 fabric widths
5 cornmeal—2 fabric widths

2. Mark fabric center. Referring to Chart A on page 36, weave 1 length of Aruba sea from center of Row 1 to side edge. Turn fabric upside down and weave remaining yarn from center to opposite side edge.

3. Noting overlaps, follow sequence indicated on charts and repeat with remaining rows. Turn charts upside down and weave next 7 rows to complete design band. The floats with asterisks accommodate 2 strands of yarn.

4. Allowing no rows of floats (1 row total) between design bands, work 4 additional design bands, 2 on each side of first design band.

5. Refer to General Instructions for finishing techniques and finish as desired. ❖

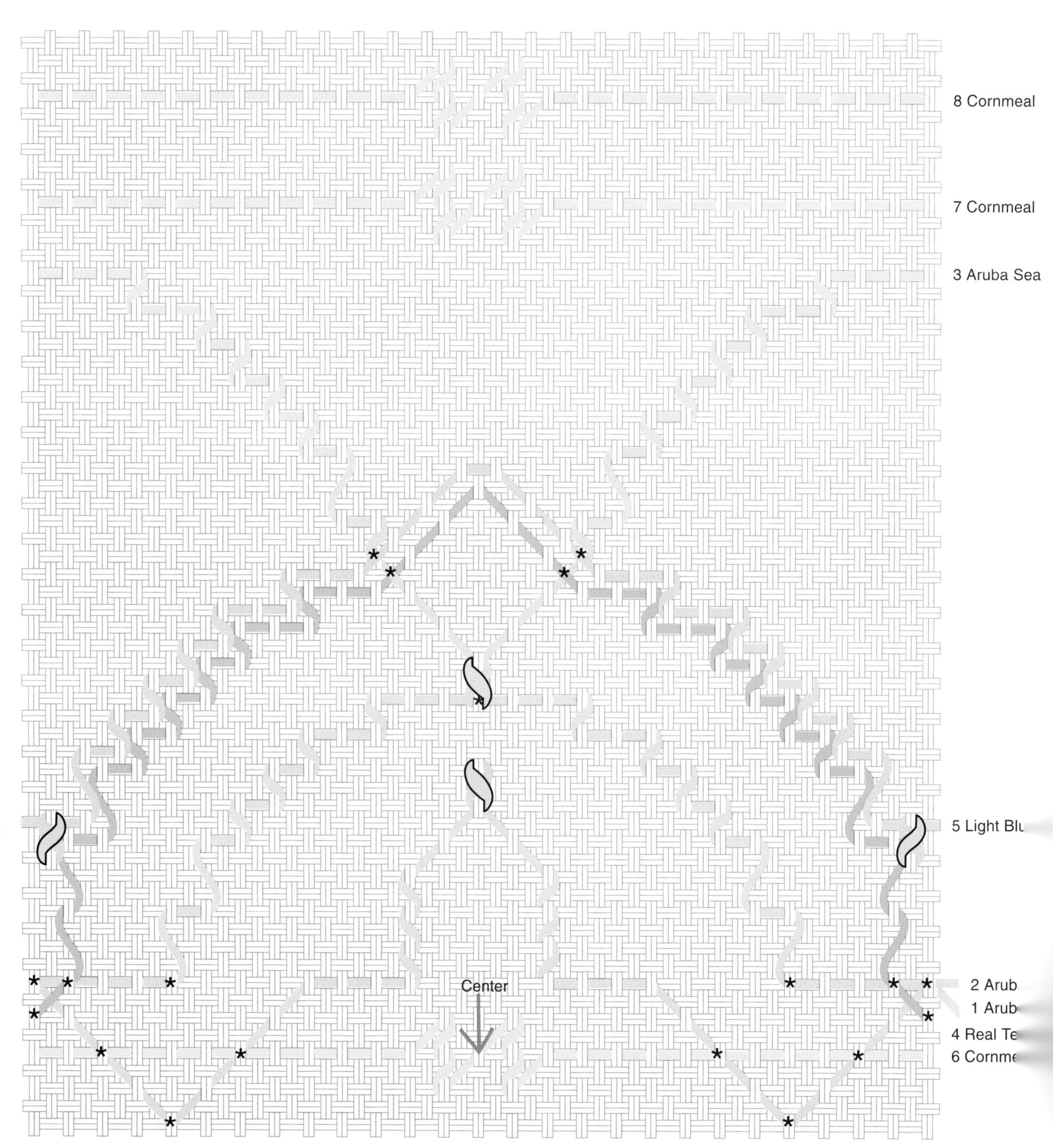
8 Cornmeal
7 Cornmeal
3 Aruba Sea
5 Light Blu
Center
2 Arub
1 Arub
4 Real Te
6 Cornme

Chart A

Pumpkin Spice Throw

Display this fall-colored throw over your sofa or snuggle up in your favorite outdoor chair to enjoy the crisp, cool fall days.

Skill Level
Easy

Finished Size
53 inches x 70 inches

Materials
- Monk's cloth:
  2½ yds natural
- Red Heart Super Saver medium (worsted) weight yarn (7 oz/364 yds/198g per skein):
  1 skein #254 pumpkin
- #13 yarn needle

Pattern Notes
Refer to General Instructions for preparing monk's cloth and for stitching information.

Instructions
1. For each design band you will need the following yarn lengths:
4 lengths—4 fabric widths

2. Mark fabric center. Referring to chart on page 40, weave 1 length from center of Row 1 to side edge. Turn fabric upside down and weave remaining yarn from center to opposite side edge.

3. Repeat with remaining row. Turn chart upside down and weave next 2 rows to complete design band. Note that the floats with the asterisks accommodate two strands of yarn.

4. Allowing 12 rows of floats (25 rows total) between design bands, work 4 additional design bands, 2 on each side of first design band.

5. Refer to General Instructions for finishing techniques and finish as desired. ❖

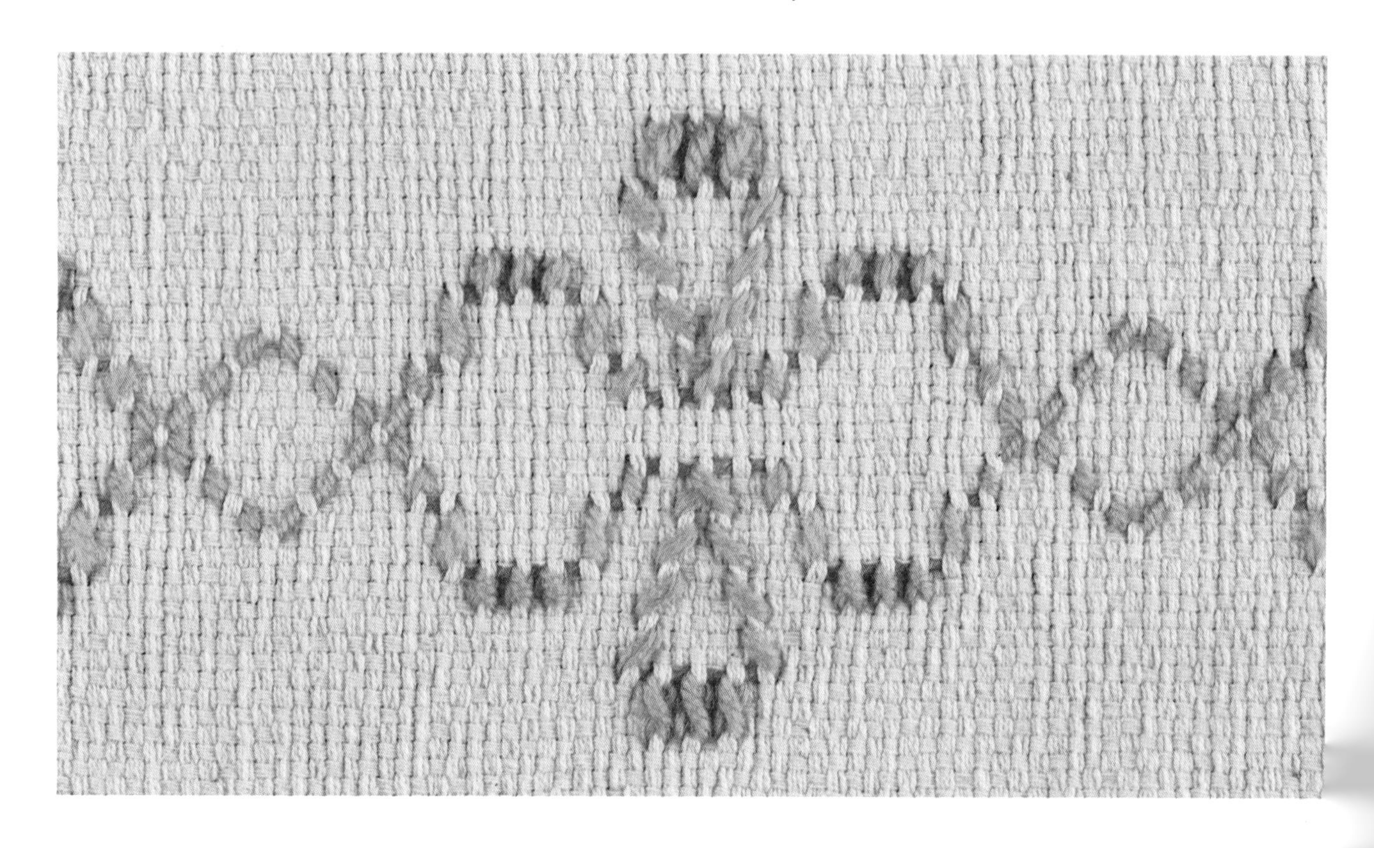

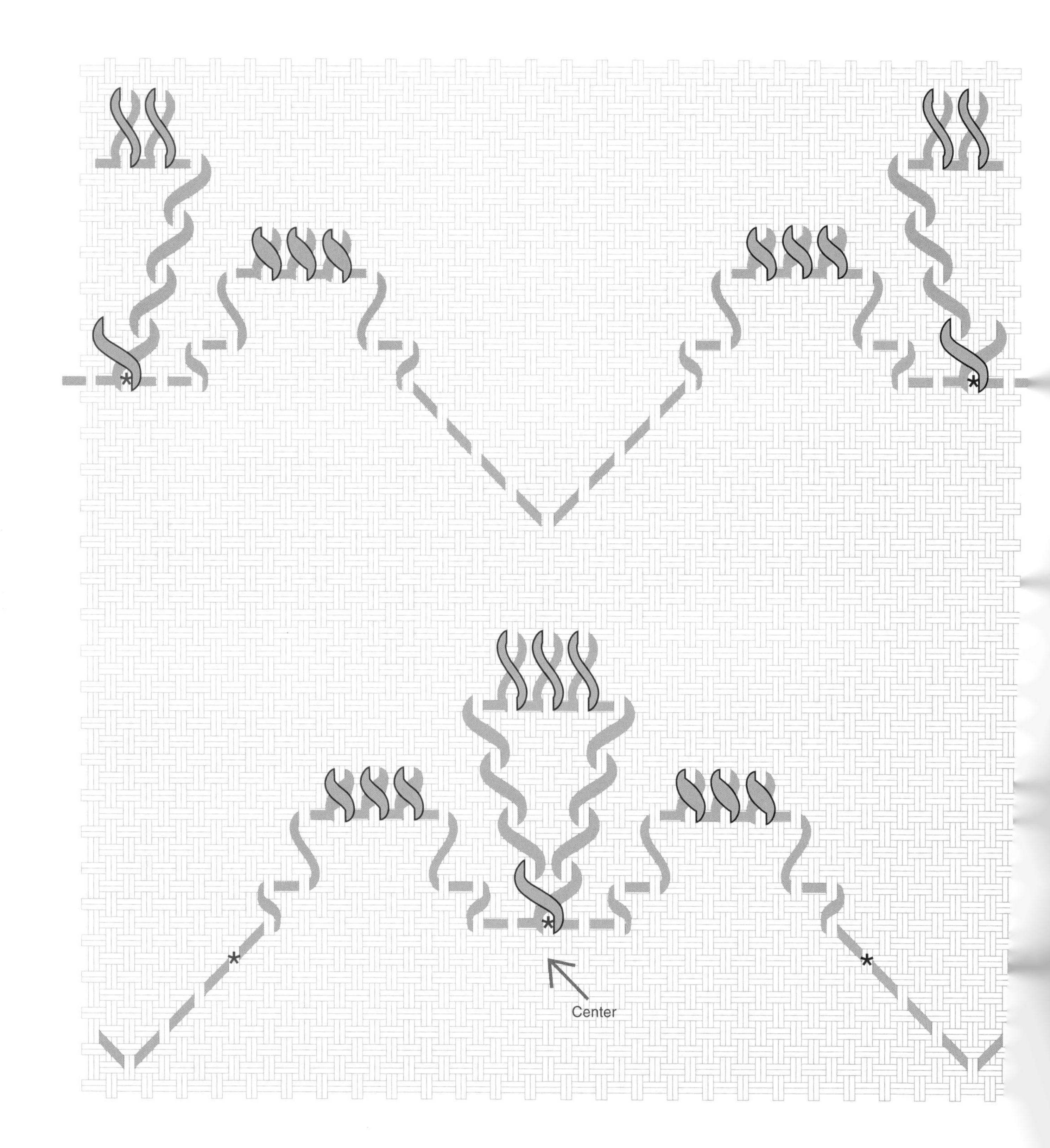
Center

Argyle Diamonds Throw

Add a splash of color to any room with this beautiful throw.

Skill Level
Easy

Finished Size
47½ inches x 64 inches

Materials
- Monk's cloth:
  2½ yds natural
- Annie's Choice medium (worsted) weight yarn (7 oz/328 yds/198g per skein):
  1 skein each #AC1000 garnet red and #AC1009 goldenrod
- #13 yarn needle

Pattern Notes
Refer to General Instructions for preparing monk's cloth and for stitching information.

Instructions
1. For each design band you will need the following yarn lengths:
2 garnet red—2½ fabric widths
or 2 goldenrod—2½ fabric widths

2. Mark fabric center. Referring to chart on page 45, weave 1 length of goldenrod from center to side edge. Turn fabric upside down and weave remaining yarn from center to opposite side edge. Turn chart upside down and weave next row to complete design band. The floats with asterisks accommodate 2 strands of yarn.

3. Allowing 0 rows of floats (0 rows total) between design bands, work 4 design bands with garnet red, 1 design band with goldenrod and 4 design bands with garnet red on each side of center design band.

4. Refer to General Instructions for finishing techniques and finish as desired. ❖

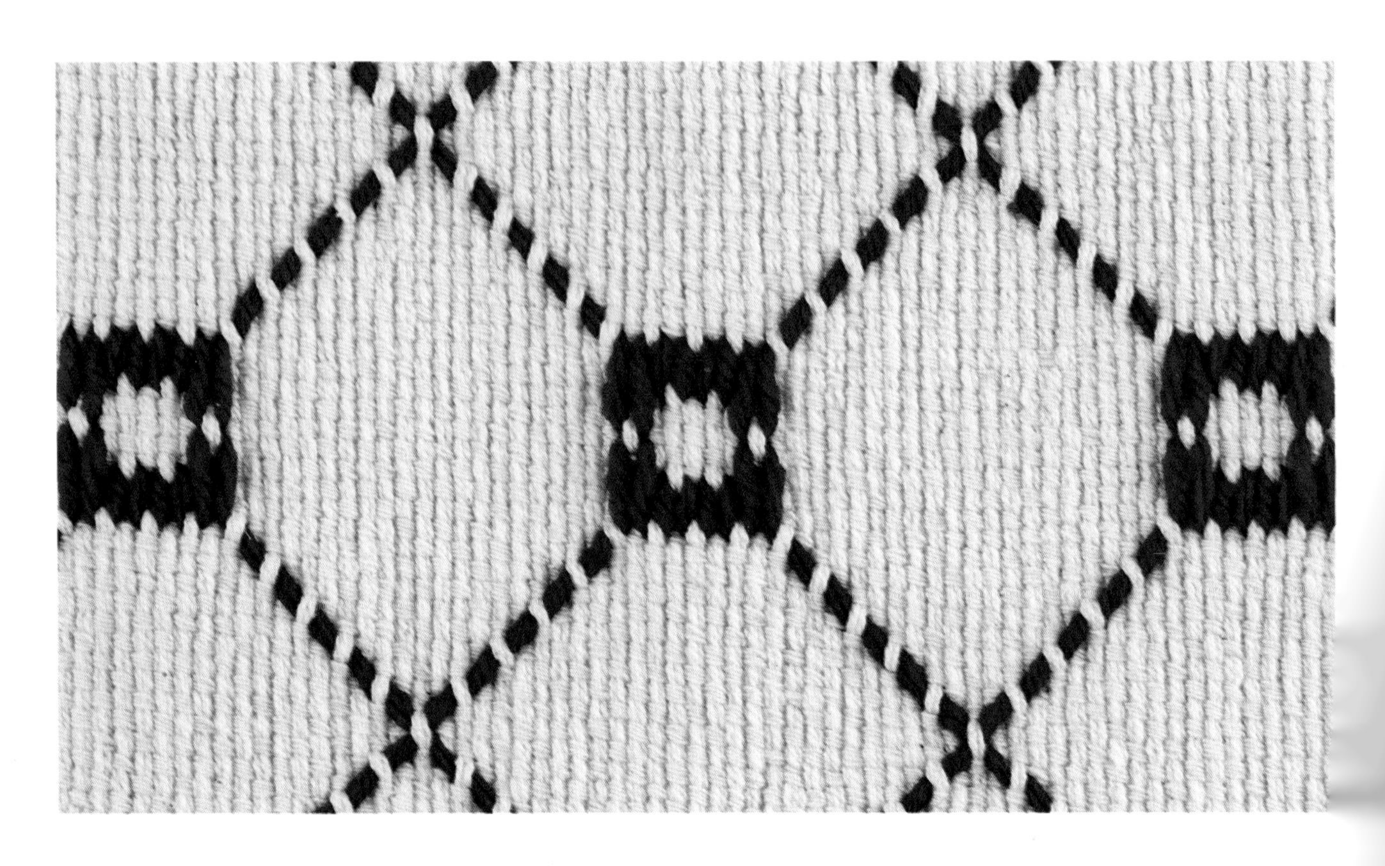

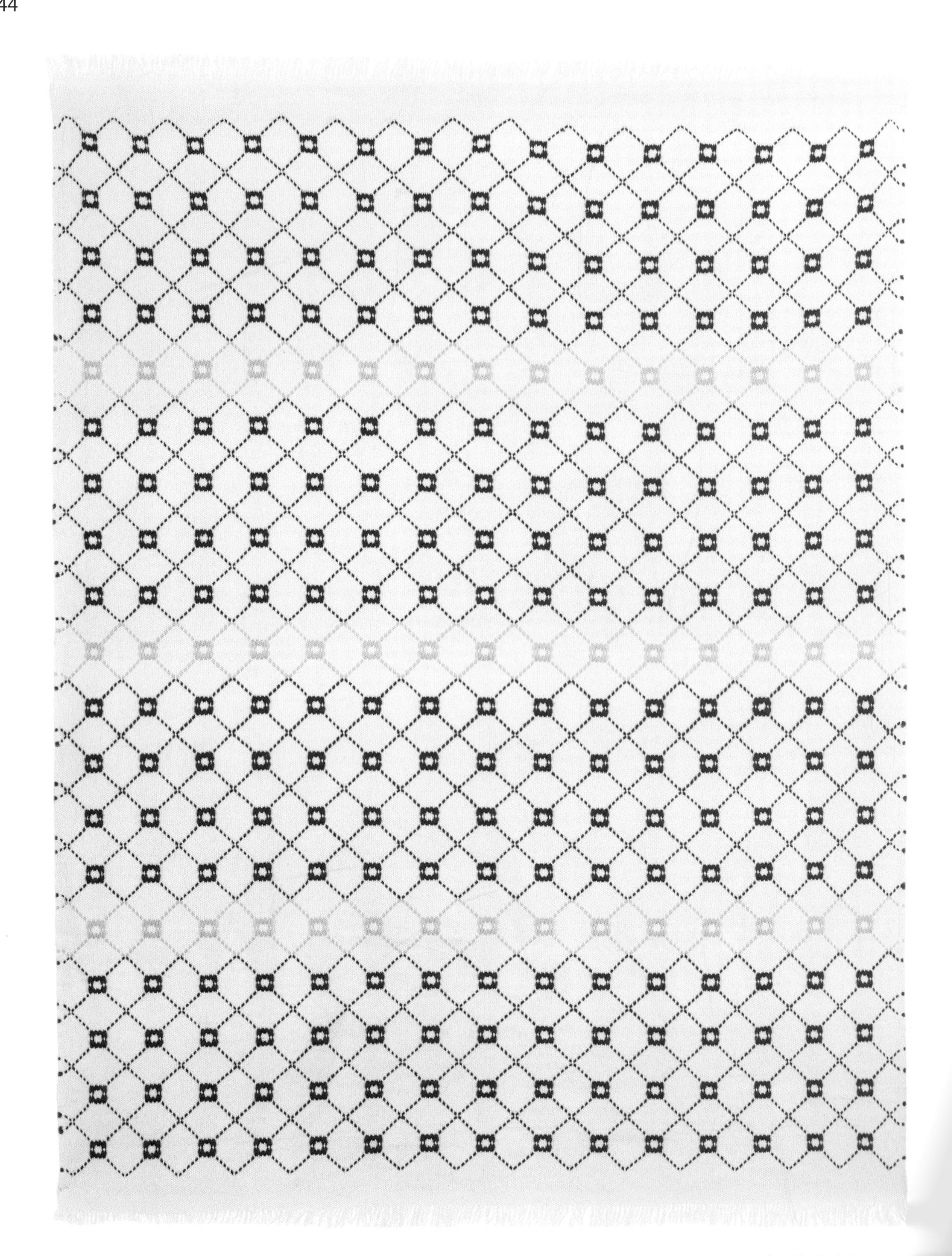

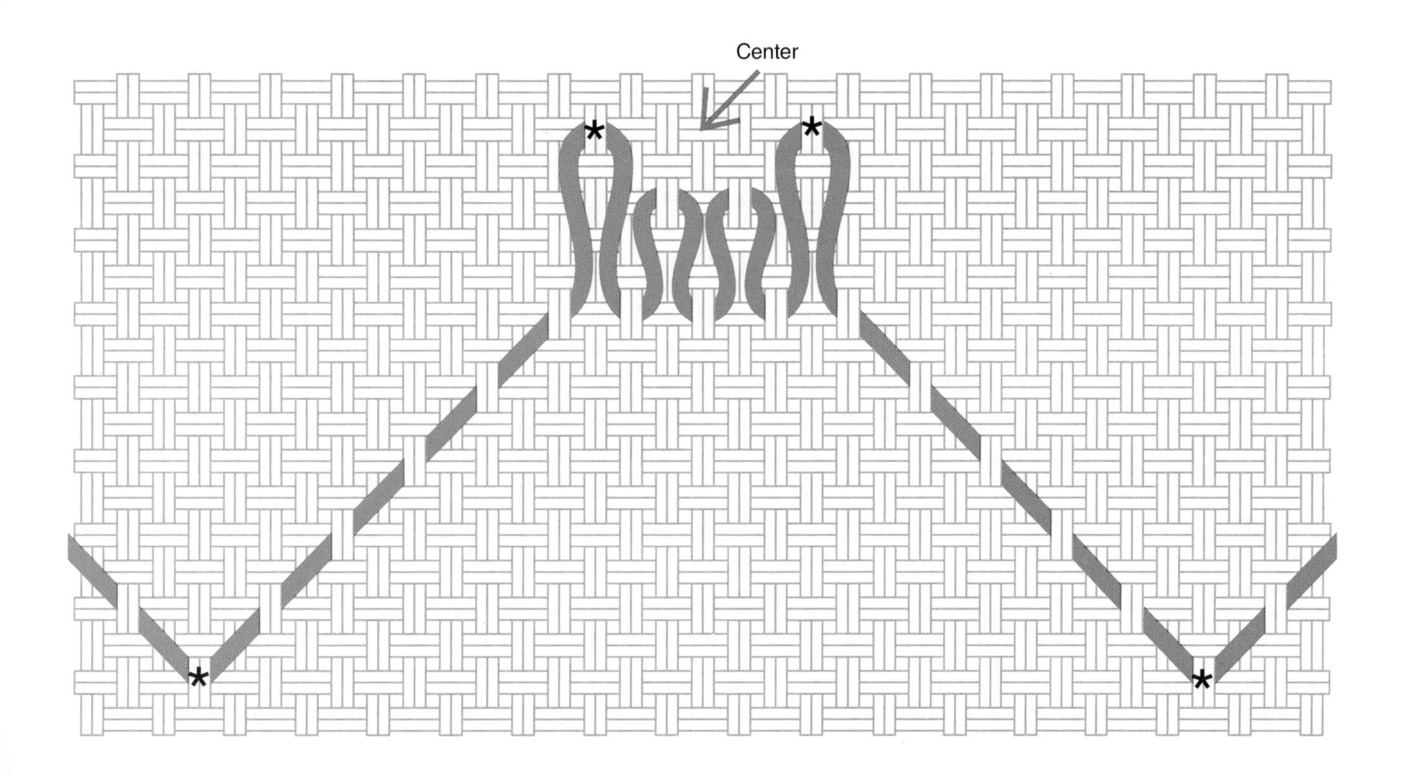

Monk's Cloth and yarn can be purchased at AnniesAttic.com

Monk's Cloth for Today is published by DRG, 306 East Parr Road, Berne, IN 46711. Printed in USA.

RETAIL STORES: If you would like to carry this pattern book or any other DRG publications, visit DRGwholesale.com

Every effort has been made to ensure that the instructions in this pattern book are complete and accurate. We cannot, however, take responsibility for human error, typographical mistakes or variations in individual work. Please visit AnniesCustomerCare.com to check for pattern updates.

ISBN: 978-1-59217-371-6
1 2 3 4 5 6 7 8 9

House of White Birches, Berne, Indiana 46711 AnniesAttic.com

Other Monk's Cloth books available from House of White Birches.

- 21312 *Monk's Cloth Afghans for Christmas*
- 21295 *Learn To Make Monk's Cloth Afghans*

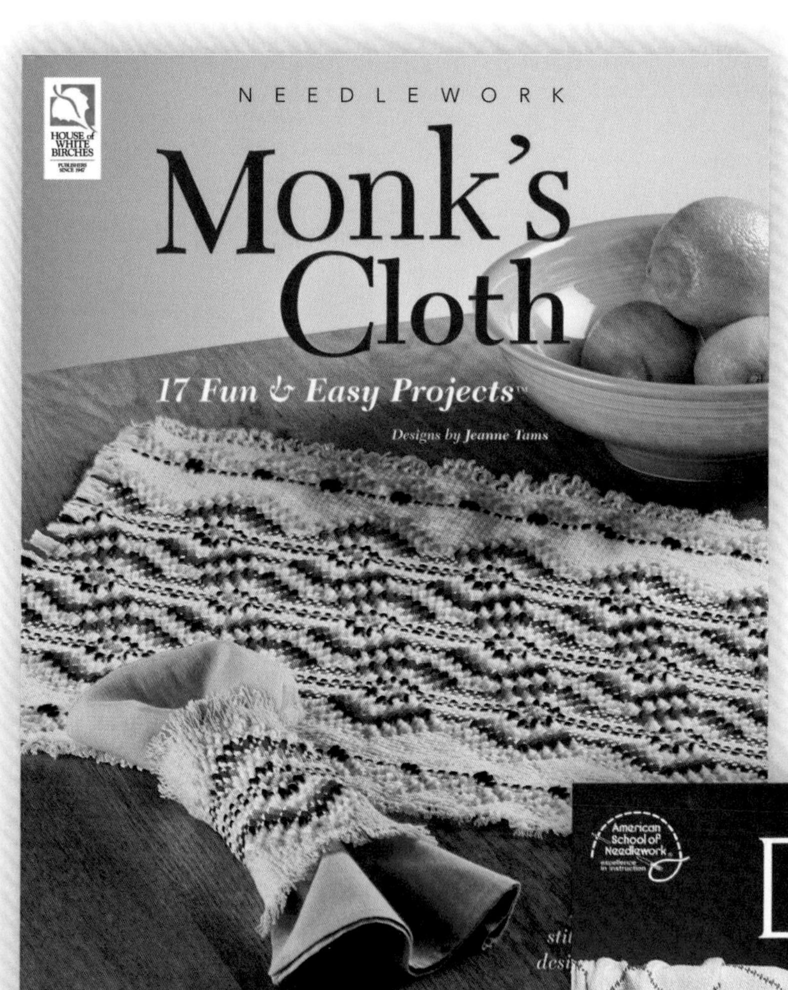

- 291010 *Monk's Cloth 17 Fun & Easy Projects*
- 21327 *Monk's Cloth Diamond Afghans*

Available at AnniesAttic.com

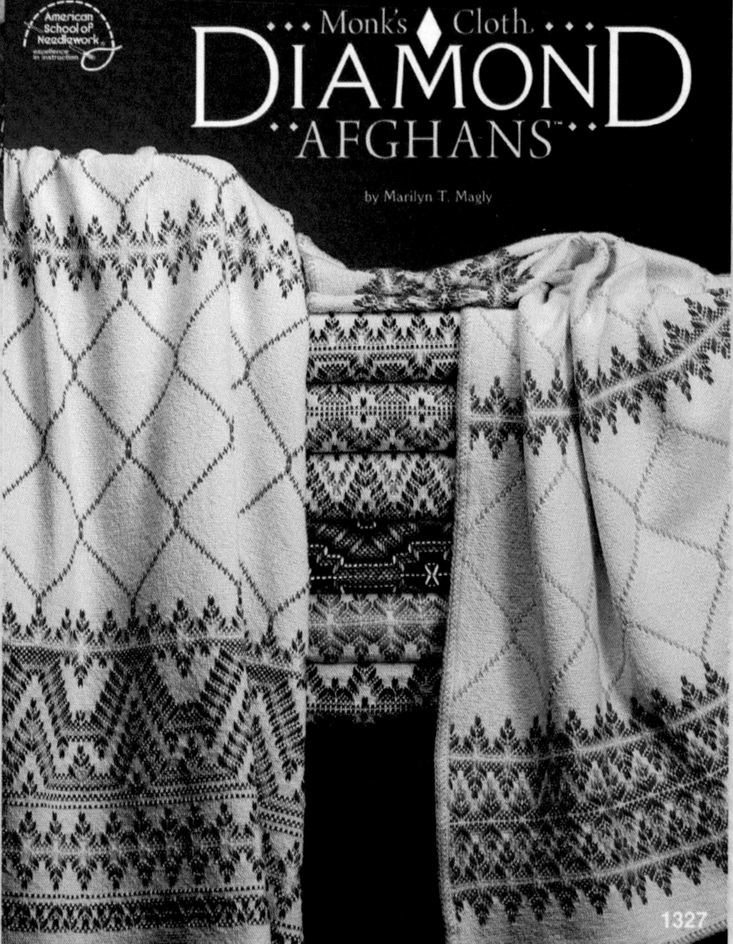

Photo Index

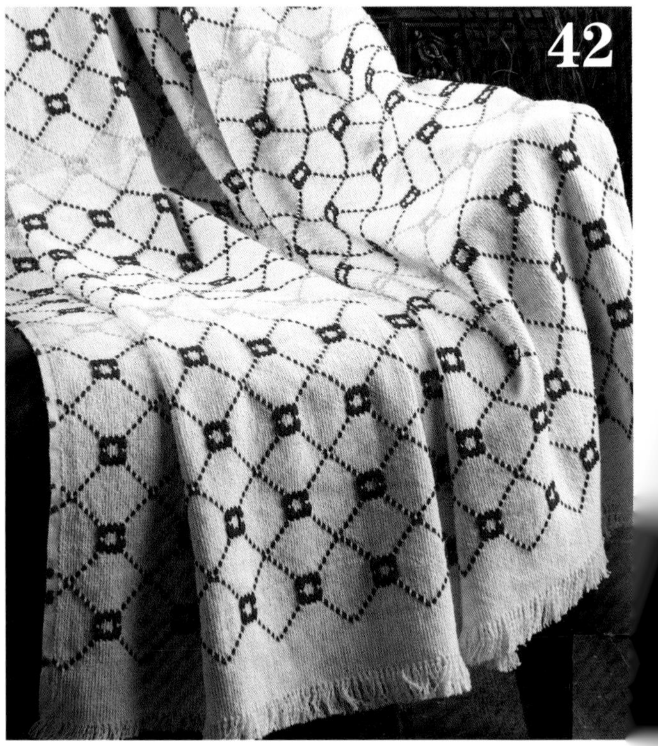